THIS COUNTRY IS NOT A POEM

POEMS

Kraftgriots
Also in the series (POETRY)

David Cook et al: *Rising Voices*
Olu Oguibe: *A Gathering Fear*; winner, 1992 All Africa Okigbo prize for Literature & Honourable mention, 1993 Noma Award for Publishing in Africa
Nnimmo Bassey: *Patriots and Cockroaches*
Okinba Launko: *Dream-Seeker on Divining Chain*
Onookome Okome: *Pendants*, winner, 1993 ANA/Cadbury poetry prize
Nnimmo Bassey: *Poems on the Run*
Ebereonwu: *Suddenly God was Naked*
Tunde Olusunle: *Fingermarks*
Joe Ushie: *Lambs at the Shrine*
Chinyere Okafor: *From Earth's Bedchamber*
Ezenwa-Ohaeto: *The Voice of the Night Masquerade*, joint-winner, 1997 ANA Cadbury poetry prize
George Ehusani: *Fragments of Truth*
Remi Raji: *A Harvest of Laughters*, joint-winner, 1997 ANA/Cadbury poetry prize
Patrick Ebewo: *Self-Portrait & Other Poems*
George Ehusani: *Petals of Truth*
Nnimmo Bassey: *Intercepted*
Joe Ushie: *Eclipse in Rwanda*
Femi Oyebode: *Selected Poems*
Ogaga Ifowodo: *Homeland & Other Poems*, winner, 1993 ANA poetry prize
Godwin Uyi Ojo: *Forlorn Dreams*
Tanure Ojaide: *Delta Blues and Home Songs*
Niyi Osundare: *The Word is an Egg* (2000)
Tayo Olafioye: *A Carnival of Looters* (2000)
Ibiwari Ikiriko: *Oily Tears of the Delta* (2000)
Arnold Udoka: *I am the Woman* (2000)
Akinloye Ojo: *In Flight* (2000)
Joe Ushie: *Hill Songs* (2000)
Ebereonwu: *The Insomniac Dragon* (2000)
Deola Fadipe: *I Make Pondripples* (2001)
Remi Raji: *Webs of Remembrance* (2001)
'Tope Omoniyi: *Farting Presidents and Other Poems* (2001)
Tunde Olusunle: *Rhythm of the Mortar* (2001)
Abdullahi Ismaila: *Ellipsis* (2001)
Tayo Olafioye: *The Parliament of Idiots: Tryst of the Sinators* (2002)
Femi Abodunrin: *It Would Take Time: Conversation with Living Ancestors* (2002)
Nnimmo Bassey: *We Thought It Was Oil But It Was Blood* (2002)
Ebi Yeibo: *A Song For Tomorrow and Other Poems* (2003)
Adebayo Lamikanra: *Heart Sounds* (2003)
Ezenwa-Ohaeto: *The Chants of a Minstrel* (2003), winner, 2004 ANA/NDDC poetry prize and joint-winner, 2005 NLNG Literature prize
Seyi Adigun: *Kàlákìní: Songs of Many Colours* (2004)
Joe Ushie: *A Reign of Locusts* (2004)

THIS COUNTRY IS NOT A POEM
POEMS

Aj. Dagga Tolar

kraftgriots

Published by

Kraft Books Limited
6A Polytechnic Road, Sango, Ibadan
Box 22084, University of Ibadan Post Office
Ibadan, Oyo State, Nigeria
✆ 02–8106655, 0804 210 8712
E-mail: kraftbooks@yahoo.com

© Aj. Dagga Tolar 2005

First published 2006

ISBN 978–039–146–0

All Rights Reserved

First printing, January 2006

Dedication

for

Christopher Okigbo
(1932-1967)

and

Rotimi Ewebiyi
(1962- 2004)

for falling down
without failing the future

Preface

How love turns up itself in its very letters into hate, and hate into love in relating to a country where nothing whatsoever works. How can one bring oneself to speak of love for one's own country, when only the few members of an already closed circle of a clique can love? To them is given the power, the power to live fulfilled, to them is everything that makes living worthy of the title life, to them alone is given the means to love, and love they love this country, I tell you they do ... and I am not pained they do, except that in keeping faith with the principle of love, charity demands from them that they share with the rest of us the good of love ... mark my words not the goods of love, but the good of being good, how we must love those who daily harm us, denying us our right to life, the rightful right of wanting to feel happy with another human and share everything flesh with another human flesh, how we fear for the greatest of all human joy — a new life, when we see all around how kids can no longer go to school ... water unaffordable to so many... how the night condemns us, eating us up from half our lifespan on the account of the fact that the sun is the only available light ... how the oil from our own soil is priced from the Manhattan of Wall Street by those who would not pay the wages of the very stock exchange from which they make their bidding...

This is the only love that is love in my country, and yet we cannot do without love, we still make love, we make babies, both wanted and most unwanted, as we fall victim over and over again to the power of the animal in us to express its art to write, to pour ink, to lie back flat and moan and murmur unintelligible words nonstop ... aiding the bid of flesh consumption. All this we do unmindful of the realities that serve to restrain our desires... We are animals and to that reign of animal, that would not give up on us, despite our flight from the cave to erecting scrapers in the sky, to our flying machines in space in search of proof of our intelligence, or is it that we are the only intelligent, all in a way impact to source this collection of poems...that part in our being that places us against so many odds and yet we are out there everyday looking out for a way, refusing the facts of other existence both in and around us and before our eyes, that from our country to the common human na *nothing nothing*. Against this very conviction, year in year out confirmed and internalized into our consciousness, we choose not to fail our mind, if we must remain sane, we tell ourselves that we would make it, it is only a question of time, the very time that is not ours, the very times without numbers that we have proclaimed that this country is finished.

What cannot be finished is life, from being unwanted beings we turn to become wanted, for how else can we live than to want to be loved by those who are made out to love us, for without us loving them they would really be finished, finished along with their system that is kept daily alive on greed, finished along with their self-rule of themselves alone. Finish them off, for life to be renewed...

If only the whole lot of us can gain this understanding to finish them off, before they finish us off ... Of course they would never finish us all, they court us, turn us against us, so as to keep some of us, for without us, how then can they honour the demand of their faith to love us more than they can love themselves ... and in turn we must love those who rule us, who against their own wishes were forced to mount the saddle and compelled to rule over us, what greater gratitude can we shower on this exemplary love of all time than to love them and this country in return.

So they bid us to love from our very beginning, a law we cannot but obey, for in turning into flesh, we ourselves mouth the word love to mean what they teach us to mean love, so never is love allowed to be love, for our lives are guided and guarded in thought and in act by fear, this fear in turn infects our word with lies, for only in turning art into lies do we become faithful and feel secure and safe in the cocoon of a country that rewards such inanities as celebrative acts that demand the accolade of all, so hearts get broken either way, as we hold on to faith only in ourselves, only in our wanting our own care, so long we get our own heart desires, all rules of decency, we break them all, so the dreams of trust of others in us and on us die, humans like us become their own shadows, unable to pick themselves up again to truly live.

But always must find a way from its too many possibilities to continue its claim to love, every turn, every street, and these many in more numbers than the many there are, get upturned into impossibilities; love unmade, love unsuccessful, love betrayed, heart broken to make you close mind and body to love. And some men go on blaming women for the mere fact of a she that names a country a woman, even when in reality, they own little or nothing of the country. We make them stretch full body before the pocket of men to earn any of the means to life. So what choice then, than to seize on love to pocket men and go on living, even for the mere fact of being alive? So this country, not the woman, for the country leaves and turns all we care for, love, to pain all through and through. So love that should turn out to be true love for ever living in happiness is frittered away on the account of the failure of this country to meet us even in the minimal with our basic needs...

Those who manage faith in full pretence, only have for themselves, the carcass of an empty coffin. They glorify the fact of a ring on their finger, a home with kids as in their own imagination, the proof of love, they are loved, they in turn also love, when in actual fact they are only busy returning to the animal we thought we had left behind when we became human. How good this is, it does honour to the very letters and spirit of the love the country demands from us, for without it, we are not a people, we are not a country.

Now that it is clear we cannot choose or make our own country, we take what the fathers of this country have fashioned out in the very depth of their wisdom and love for us. So as a matter of first rule, they bring us up with the need to love, they compel us to pledge our whole being to the country, so that everything remains for all times as usual, they forget how everything in nature is made in time to turn the other way opposite against itself. Also they forget words and meanings, our own human craft that list an antonym to every word, unfortunately for them their logic and philosophy of existence, sees everything in nature as distinct, M is M and W is W, and M cannot be the same as W, they refuse to see that M can be made to become W and W can be made to become M and this is exactly what the system foists on us. Good for us they dare cannot see that all is already on the reverse that in teaching us to love this country, since we cannot have another country, they have also taught us to hate the rule of those who make us not to want to love this country, only in this kind of love that is at the same time hate, only in this kind of hate, that is at the same time love, can we find the true love, to love this country in a collection of poems titled *This Country is not a Poem*.

For only when we have gathered words in the appropriate meaning and senses to fill the people pinned down to hating existence to feel the need and thinking that this country can be renewed, only then can we gather the acts and begin the process, the struggle to make this country a country for all, only after then can the poet find art and people woven into new poems lettered in a new existence consummating a new life of sweet love, not *This Country is Not a Poem*.

Contents

Dedication	5
Preface	6
I want to learn to say no	11
My heart is smoking	12
Loneheartedness	13
Heart handed out	14
The heart is not unmade	15
Can heal your heart	16
The heart of your open door	17
I cannot read you this poem	18
This morning	19
Deadend to poetry	20
A dying lingua	21
Disobedience of words	22
These two defy life	23
We make words	24
The tyranny of capital	25
Question stones	26
Cannot detain the poem II	27
Unfinishing the poem	28
At 2 poems	29
Forking love	30
Waste one's whole life on love	31
Found him to be your prison	32
The colour of death	33
The blast	34
Hungered by hate	35
Endangering poetry	36
Cannot detain the poem I	37
Dying in the head	38
What pain	39
The wall is crying	40
The empire never... you cease it out of you	41

They can't pain you out of love	45
How do you tell of my people to your people	47
The leaf leaves over	49
Too lust to life	50
Another May 15	52
A colony calling for the last verser	53
The Efuala from Efualand	58
Love no longer a poem	60
This country is not a poem	61
How can we count	69
Love another name for murder	70
Reading of love	71
The way to hate	72
The ashes of the heart	73
Unwrite God	74

I want to learn to say no

I want to learn to say No
To your flesh
But inkful my pen-is
Stretchful to spell

Out a poem and pour
Your flesh
All the letters you want
From me

I cannot be Okigbo
Meaning fail my own word of No
Before the rock of your eyes
Stealing into me

Stirs all hair in me straight
Cannot bear a pebble
Only when the gag is back place
And uptight is rest

And words settle to their truth
Can poetry begin …
Only then can this poem write
What I don't want to do

For words to lay down the lies
My love cannot hold
I want to learn to say No
To your flesh

My heart is smoking
(Efemena)

My heart is smoking, not
Yet fire
The higher

Burns the need for no other
But you alone
Yet you bone

But how long to me can my
Water hold
Freely sold

Me to visit for freedom on the flesh
Of hell' way
And always

My heart gets the burn, love
Without the art
Leaves the heart

Falling, falling down to hell
My sin
Is not loving gin

But you
And only you
My heart is smoking…

Loneheartedness

My heart is plucked packed ready for delivery
Only worry is my hands too blood neat
Words too white in tongue to harm
Another with heart like me
So to sob of tears I commit
My unhooked to live on
The freedom if free to
Be another word for
A loneheartedness

Heart handed out

Heart handed out — on lips
Pact
Not words called to witness
Moaning
Of return to our speechless state
Animal
Is all there is to thrust forth the
Heart
Cannot spell letters cannot fear
Fear
Sucking deep into the lips for fun
Both
Leaping from flesh back to lip
Mouthful
Chewing up the heart is
Swallowed

The heart is not unmade

Eyes shut. How then can the heart
See Redblood from Red
Figure the feel of flesh
The face
Uncalculated is no error
No arms way out
For without leave love can
For with living always is with a leaving
A harm the heart is not unmade
Even with eyes — only to see
The lies of letters
Words
What! Is art
A way for legs to be always
Two and trod in three
To be a tree and root to countless spot
The care of the heart is motion

Can heal your heart

Why cast your lot for love
In the cold of crossing oceans
On words of wait

When before you is fulfilment
Destiny

Why look out to the mountains
And worry your pretty eyes
Watching for the stars to land

When already on this land
Is this hill I am
Can heal your heart

All times with love
Seek no further

The heart of your open door
(Pat Egedegu)

In captive
To your heart
Already I am charmed

To find
Love lost way
In flesh and smile in you

Can mean
Nothing else
But love

Favoured I am
To be with you yourself
And you

To be the one
I want to close the heart
Of your open door

Only to after dawn on your coming
You return back me book
You fall me heart down

You close your face up
How you have already gone down
To your knees

The sin is not you
Na this country
That close minds

And you can only see otherwise
So I am out
The heart of your open door closed

I cannot read you this poem

I cannot read you
This poem

Help me write it
Your mind sees my pain
Every one more word I try
Suffers me to cry

Help me with your mind
Keep your lips sealed
They are yet to learn
Ban, bars, wigs and gowns

Translate soft flesh
And life to mean
Words — write on blood
Blood — this is yet our hope

That poetry cannot die
Unwritten

This morning

When the dawn does the weeping
How can the leafy face of dew
Duty any dot of due
To innocence

This morning
Like others before — gathers still
Mournings even murmuring
Sobs of dried droppings
Blocks of tears

Deadend to poetry
(Modupe Meho)

On account of your learning to write
If I have to wait, art would suffer
So I go ahead to read your lips leaping
Every line of letters a poem

How then to my language
You say you don't know many words
When all meaning is in the heart
You speak fine,

Why labour to learn to be all loved
To be held by all before
Is not to say something new
No longer your story

But stolen
What they want you to become
Like every other them
The same

This is why you are at wrestle with words
For the world to learn this story
Your story, not a new page to life
Would be deadend to poetry

A dying lingua

A dying lingua like
My mother tongue
She is still there now
My mother alive

But unable to rock
Tune me with little memories
Words with which I was nurtured
Stiffen silences

All the memorable pleasantries
Crumble down falling
No ladder on the rung
This growing wall of a country

No new letters into meaning
Unable to spend my own mother's
Language in wanting to eat, drink
Or sleep with the aid of sex

A dying lingua like
My mother's tongue
No currency cannot translate
"Money is everything in life"

Disobedience of words

And language disagrees
But with no feet to mount a calvary
Against the crusade against us
The poet *popes* a cross

To bless their instruments of sin
A loadful of nails a hammer
And their other load of poison litany
What a way to be free from sin

But for the commanding disobedience of words
To death on a cross like Christ's
To cross into a peculiar
And unseen type of speaking also is a sin

These two defy life

These words
    Birth, Death
These two defy life
    They are there
Always they are there
Reigning joy, raining tears
Meaning nothing else, but
    Birth, Death

In between the Birth, the Death
The translation not always from love
Is life
    But try then to understand
Just this word —
    Life

Becomes a birth
A walking unmindful not working or not
Feet or no fit
    To draft death
        To mean life
To lip — this then is life

Birth no longer is Birth
Death no longer is Death
See how life squeezing meaning out
But all life' retutoring
Letters go on being letters
Making these two words
Meaning

And birth and Death
Undying, the dictionary
Meaning unchanging
—The only language
We all once must speak

We make words

We make words to stew the blame
    Of everything wrong with our act
        Only for wrong to be free
            To go on on the act
                of more wrongs

Forever words would be there
    We can only like this forever
        Return to become a bubbling out stew
Cold like before the beginning
                      Then words would be free

The tyranny of capital

Whence life was with words
    Humans lived sharing
Only for the tyranny of 'CAPITAL'
      Letters from small
      Machine the greed
To be first of having everything
        All of us
Since then our own small
     Letter' basic needs
      Is scared to death
        By the STATEme(a)nt
         Order of CAPITAL

Question stones

You question stones with a throw
I laugh the laugh of cold
Storing up stones of words
To mount me on the mountain

Unknown me I am me
—The very word without which
Or no wish
You cannot hold against me

Cannot detain the poem II

They detain the Poet
Can they detain the poem
Can they?

The poem
Is not flesh
That bars can hold behind

The poem
Is not bone
That cannot break iron

The poem
Is not just the Poet
Or the life of the poet

The poem
Is everything life
Everything life breathes on

The iron, the bars
Them who detain the Poet
Dare not dream to detain

The poem
For first they must themselves
Cancel out of life

And if they do
The Poet so is free to weave
New poems

For even the Poet
Cannot detain
The poem

Unfinishing the poem

Unfinishing the poem
Is not like a wall
Dismembered
Brick by brick
In safety keeps
For remounting
New erection

The womb
Is not finished
Not the poem
World all through with words
Like the prick pulled out
The poem dies finished
Oh no!

The poem
In its finished state is born
Not of the womb–
The wall of the word
Holds the flow of the period
It stops not the conjugation
With words

At 2 poems
(For Efemena)

I cannot copulate with 2 poems
At the same time
For art is not like the heart
Arteries, veins to flow

At more than one pour
Like the pen is
But not possible at the pour
Of semen

If love can transcend two
and engage three, four
Then, let me first die

I cannot live to lie
With art —
Making effort to erase you
From inside of me

Forking love

Forking love like a tongue
Into units

Colours every word with wet
Ink of libidinal blood

Unfree from blood–the wasting
Water of life

Colours dying in a rainbow of
Failed meaning

The heart is other way
The eyes lied

So love is not for dying and so
You are leaving

To live in freedom, enjoy the joy
Remember

All is imprisoned without exempt
By dialectics

Today's sweet is the seed to sour
The pain tomorrow

Going gets better, bitter
Provoking rueful thoughts

For the tears of my cry over
Your saddening word

Hangs tightly to the eyelid unshed
I cannot cry for love

Waste one's whole life on love
(For Efemena)

How it seems a waste
One's whole life on love
And not reap in return

To then go on with love
Meaning not more
Than the letters of the name
Of this country

Is to go on mounting words
Of love like the president does
And I know his love earns us nothing
And I know what power can bring to bear

Only you don't know
Every other thing love
Cannot give is not love

Found him to be your prison
(For Serah Eloho)

We are not taking anything away
From each other
We have to our flesh given to each other
Nothing

I urge you on into the world
Without walls
If already you have found him
To be your prison

To throw away at art your freedom
I kiss my own flesh
To bid you bye…your flesh
Unable to do me

The colour of death

Red juice imprints the flesh
Bruising blues for a fever break
The heart crowds out the cloud
The white smoked into ash

Leaps on
The bloodful water
Drinking the black off the back
Of my skin

The carcassing yellow
Brokers a break away from green
To fellow a restful lay on the brown
Is sand

The colour of death

The blast

It is the blast
The blood spluttering
In the distance last
Of death lettering

Our anger at life
Nudges us to living while
Our land is rend in two by a knife
Believing

Helps us to dreams
We cannot die
Our lord lives
Bombs blast us to breathe

Hungered by hate

Hungered by hate
Eating me up to hate
Life

How can I
Express this motion
For love hates

It is life
That cannot live free from
Hunger I hate

Endangering poetry

Show me one poet
Not one hates the word

But show me one me
Who would not be fooled

To hear the Poet say
"I am the word"

Poets who with their lives
Give life to words

I know you think they know
No word begins or ends with thought

And so to my own words
Even I would not fall down

Only to be blazed all over
By fellow poets for failing

To worship the words
"I am the word"

"I am endangering
Poetry" they say

Cannot detain the poem I

The poem
Is not flesh, and bone
That can be put behind bars
That cannot break through iron
Beyond the concrete wall electrified
To kill the attemptee escapee

The poem
They cannot detain
Even if they dismember words
Into letters, can they kill thought
Would letters not intermingle
27 separate moons to incarcerate

Each letter?
One moon would still be free
Letters still would dance
Their feet to melt into words
The flesh have they not heard
Of freedom

If they dismember words
Dictatorship is dismantled
Cannot then stand
Cannot then detain
The poem

Dying in the head

How we carry ourselves
In the end
Life leaves us unliving
Fit for a cemetery

You see now
You don't see
Dreams dying in the head
Rottening up the skull

What pain

What pain
Can there be in hell
If all life
We live on

On pain
To be free from hell
After death
And never are we free

Until death
Do us free
From life
And then we can no longer feel

The pain
Life is hell
In vain to escape hell
We pain our flesh in pain to feel.

The wall is crying

Tears can no longer be water
To sea
The wall is crying
Our eyes inability to see
Our bodies sealed-in not drinking
Unable to wet out we curse water
To stone to eat sand

Only to haul all our land
Lives on the bare —
Face of a concrete floor

And tears can no longer be water
But bodies dropping
To a drying desert dripping
To see the sand back to sea
The wall is crying
And the sun is bleeding
Red eye

The empire never... You cease it out of you
(To Benjamin Zephaniah)

Benjamin was not for once lost
But his fan for words is found
Bothers all other brothers bowing
Willingly willing to "Officer" you
Maybe then as one of them
Words on their own would cajole you
To offer your black lips to kiss
The Royal handglove of the queen

How you sizedrum the Empire's hide
In your mind
Is not in their thought "you are wrong"
Again it would turn out the old order way
To take us all back behind the times
We no longer live
We no longer remember
The children of slaves picking on own skin
Soothing only on songs from the distance shores
Of one day Africa, but we know all why
The Empire came, strong from the free sweat
Of our Blackfores, so they would not ship us all
As being planting sheep we were now the cheap
Factoryhands to die out our lives
On words that heaven up our hopes
To give them life evermore luxurious
Only for the same words we still dying hanging on
We hope on hopping, as you came to see the root

Africa— the homeland of root
Natty dread dreaming to unlock Africa
Here the dreadlock is the trademark of nuts
Not nuts babble to bubbling blues
Of Christ is coming again.

This is Lagos
They would not let you see Ajegunle
The homeland is far from what your eyes have beheld
Not this comfort of Ikoyi, Victoria Island
Still named in trust for the Queen
The Empire here is alive
Why then did you come
If for Blackskin to see
What then is Brixton?

Here the empire is alive and kicking
Not with chains canalling our homeminds
The Devil flee only for cover in our own skin
Prostrating to the curse of Blackslavemasters
Cooing in pleadtones to the choicest G8's Baboons:
"Forgive us our Debt"
Against the raised voices of clenched fist
On the streets of Genoa,
Crying out our cause against their own Baboons:
"Cancel the Debts"
The law in our own homeland is the dictate
Of the Empire' wellbeing
We pay with our lives for doctrines
That brings to us the sorrows of the letter 'D'
Like dictators, deleting us with drugs, darkness
Drinking dirtwater, disease displacement
Divorce, detention, death as in Deregulation
Plying permanent pains and palaver
Perishing the lot of the people
To die under a billboard like Michael Powell
That should in truth should be reading
"As the government privatizes
Only the few rich benefit"
Is to die a death already paid for by Capital
A death far better in the heart of the Empire
For you can cry, not here in the frontiers
"This is from the President" and a moment after
A man is bombed to pieces till date unresolved

Unequalled world over our own Justice Minister
Who killed him? Dikibo, like Harry Marshal
Crimes committed by armed robbers
So say the President and who can go against
What we know is in our hearts
And without words what we know goes unsaid
As "stray bullet" and "accidental discharge"
Creed its way into official record
To account for our own common death.
Hannah Odunola Alli, Segun Savage, Idowu
Awopeju, Toyin Adelugba, Nnamdi Ekwuyasi,
Morakinyo Akerele, Hussaini Abdulkarin
Our own Michael Powells, not ten dozen
Here we cannot count
Our police stations are execution centres
Operation sweep, fire the fire
Kills only the innocent, the armless
The Empire is here and alive
Expiring us from bullet bought
With our black gold to enrich London,
New York, Paris, Berlin "enslaving us
To create their dreams"
To keep the Empire alive here

And for your dear there
The Empire also is alive in Blair's
Attempt at poetry
An anthology co-authored with Bush
A complete unpoetical collection titled:
Words of Mass Deception
And who dies, again the innocent poor
The lies for an Empire's quest for oil
Is the truth why the troops
Occupies Iraq and not this WMD
Huttoning-up a "whitewash" can only cease
Only if we learn that Empire cannot cease
You cease it out of you
Not this one – act –of – you

Alone as Benjamin, no not enough
Not when even the acts of millions
On the streets against the war
Did not stop Bush and Blair

How then can the Empire cease
See it lettered in history
Only the collective act of the people
In full blown revolt
Acting not to stop at words
But on to pluck down not just
Bush, Blair and their likes
But the very system of capital
Putting profit before people
Only then can Empire truly cease

They can't pain you out of love
(For Ben Tomoloju @ 50)

How have you managed with your eyes
These years, these scenes of an endless act
Of ART is not meaning
To live all for the ART
To be 50

In this country of wrath
Six less than you
44 to waste
1914 to blame for black blood fiasco
Now black gold flood
And they still steal fire
Skinning us off red to flow our blood
To moisture the mud to brick our body

The anthill is mounting millions of ants
In a descent
Rush to be crushed to the uprooted
Cross of Christ
And yet break bond with his very words
For how can we go on without bread
And not choose to feed on wood
So no shelve stand
No shadow to showcase us
And yet we still dance
Yokolu yokolu ko wa ton bi
It is not finished here

Not when you have opened your eyes
Lived to keep a dream for thunder
In young hearts alive
Remember Okigbo
The prophecy of the Poet
Consumed him chasing
After his own words

The Elephant is still standing
This carcass of a country
Eating up dreams
Multiplying wants our own minted notes
Can't buy
How then does one now care for a drum
Ebami bi Beni
Hiding meaning only the FEET can hear

The devil is a cross in my heart
Dictators deregulated by dem dey crase
I cannot fear hell or its gun
We have seen it all boomed
GBOLAKA
They can't pain you out of love
For the ART, no they just can't
Not with all the ART you craft
Winning us away from despair
Preparing us anew to make love
Like you with ART

How do you tell of my people to your people
(For Jill Morgan)

Massa still dey chop O
Na white before before
Now na Black O
Black White Black
White Black White
Na Massa still dey chop O
The people still dey cry O

Throngs of hate fire tears this land
Tongues forever in battle against other lips
In wait to win the saltwater drops of faces' tears
Our only clean drop of free water
Supplied rich This country
Hungering on on sadness
Tell me, can your soul
Keep away from thirst
When even your own eye saltwater
No matter how rainful
Prepaid to network Igbadun*
To the lapping tongues of
— the very powerful

Repeat chorus

This story
How do you tell of my people to your people
Our skin deepness paints our hearts
Black, then is why nothing works
But how can black not work
Were not Blacks
The slaves sold to sun the soil

---

* *Yoruba word for enjoyment.*

The fruit growth market to marble
The Whiteman's world to worship
And sing: "In God we trust"
God, a new name for money enthroned
Civilization can do without shedding blood
Not machine–in need also of red palm oil
We Blacks planted
Only for the: "Maxim and Gatling Guns"
To leap us of our labour and land
And reap us from us

Repeat chorus

Then and now
Changing colour, not changed
Gained the land
No fire shot the flag won
Fires millions of our people anew
A new land, a new beginning
Commandeering on — in chief
Na thief

But whose fashion
They wear the uniform
Our great-grandfathers sang against
"Oomore ondi soja
Agbe bon sori" * (x2)
Dispensing off the people's need
Who is first to send the congratulation
When we still scream out "rigged rigged"
In telling of my people to your people
Tell them the same Massa of the whiteman's land
They rule this land as before
Through the way we think to rule

The leaf leaves over
(For Rotimi Ewebiyi, 1962–2004)

Leaves *over* like a leaf
At every turn to leave
A new day unable before you
I cannot count my tears
The dripping drops of my tears
Leaves over on the leaf
The very birth of thee
Cased out in carcass, green–
Golden, we could only have dreamed
Our together till the last day to triumph
Over our common foes the capitalists
Whose greedy lives penury us to death

Oh, how is this same death a sickness
Another name for Capital to cage us out short of you
They who fail us all, your life
Was all meaning to us in the struggle
Against them who pile up
Capital in millions of cashnotes
While millions go on in hunger
How you have guided many
To the path of Red to rage anger
In full meaning of class struggle

More like Sveldov to us
Your place no other name can fill
In our hearts to be RE
Can only mean for us that we REmain
Like you to the end committed
Like Marx, Engels, Lenin, Trotsky
To struggle and rally on the working people
To destined history, anew
For none to live in want or need
For none to live in quest for the greed
When truly 'workers of the world unite' to rule

Too lust to life
(Edward Adeleke)

Too lust to life to want to die
For love consigned to care over the remains
Is a passage placed out of life
Unable to find a body
For God in Genesis
Did not author was authored not by love
But by our life

To know we we God God a meet
A red line error for a double — so delete one we
And the first God then stands on the latter God —
Our story
What is not a myth is not love
What is love is not a myth
Jesus
To find me is to turn me out of life
I found a way to live
Unable to retain love for life' remains
And life rends out of the body
Believe

For the soul is —so no care then
For the body believe
And the world falls on into the pit
Uncertain of the millions and certain
Millions for the few
Agreeing much I know you do of the script
For struggle,
If only I can with you like you believe
But go on grow on books into a tree
A church
Begin to gather others but not me
My path is chosen for life

I am too lust to life to want to die before

The why then I can't with you seek salvation
See the light on the edge —
After death
No eyes to see
The body out of life
And the world falls on into the pit
Believe
Life is the soul, so what care can for the body

Another may 15
(Ifeanyi-Chukwu B.)

I know I want you
For your love
Is also my love
We share the same starvation

But after every meal fill of flesh
Comes what to do with the rest of life
We have gone our separate before
Aparting ourselves to others

Only to turn back on the past
To now living this good
This feeling that is all rich
How then we go to keep to the other down

Or is that we are in lust
For gleams of our gone by days of together
Momentary feelings of our lost past
Or your today's pain in prison

In need of relieve
Forgive my manner of thought
But where do we go?
Back to what is not working for you

Am I reclaimable
Can I keep you not to go
With me unable to have a home ready
What is the future to see

Ends in a second May 15
And like you, came pouring my heart open
Rich for full to love
Again your absence, emptying me out vacant

A colony calling for the last verser
(For Wole Soyinka @ 70)

Can we replicate like you
And not die verses
Like this country a vase
Full of 40 fools falling
G-B-A-G-A-D-A
Into smithereens
An act for a new poem
To another birth

Is why life…is.
Verse*plicate* then the same lines
For this country
Tell me who writes it

The unwasted wasting us
The sowed unsowing us
And we are not in between
A colony calling for a last Verser

Unable to write words like you
Or act again like you
On a radio station
Warning of a future coming

They didn't heed your drama
How then can we …
Stillbirthed into this dome
Called this country

Replugged into life for unexistence
How would our Yeah not be YEAA*
You call it "rottenness"
But this is life

---

* Youth Earnestly Ask Abacha

And we have no other country
We have known no other poetry
Except the gobbledegook gulped into us
From which we grope for words whose wishes–

Die us before our coming to birth

We cannot count
Who write words to waste weselves way
Out of life like Kolosa Kargbo
Verses never published

Very unlike Sesan Ajayi
His pen flew fire flies to burst out anger
His songs we can no longer
Remember on our lips

Even the living like
St. Loius Okoro Safar — hang
Words in wait for mythology
To do for us our essence

With what strength then
Can we pin down reality
Tumble (its head-up from)
Its legs-up to down

We are greying richer in pain
To pain us to the birth of more words
We cannot write
We bow before your full blown silver hair

We are poorer in all but in pain
It is words and letters
Unable to earn us a living
That have failed and not us

Unmindful—
We go on making poems
Chop open our veins

To vanity them
This generation of poets
Unable to own only but a free copy
Unread
Mugged like all in a hole

But unable like others to hide saving
To the generator of noise
Abiku constant like NEPA
Defies death to die back to die

With what eye then can we read
In this underground
Dungeon of darkness
Perfect hour of lovemaking

With whom ... poets
Born losers
Oh no!
The world is wiser and older
Than words

Even love submits
To the capital creed of cash and carry
Conjugation for our pen is
Therefore on and with paper

To pour on another flesh
And chance a new life to birth
Is to add bitterness to the bitter leaf
Of words

From which even one cannot feed

Ati ye...
Ati bo...
Lowo
Kikoro ewuro

Loro
Di kokoko...
Oro okoro...
Le lenu gbenu re sa*

There is nothing new
In these verses
Nothing therein that thought
Had not before brought forth

To therefore call for another Verser
Is to mock and make the art cry
With what hands can we dry
These tears

When with words
Hands cannot write
How then can we feel the need
For freedom

For blood to rain
When in this reigning
We are sucked
Water is extremely expensive

Blood is cheap
Our eyes is… dripping
Our blood is weeping
The living testament of this generation

Of free songs of palaver
From all….
The bargain to nothing, for free
And then who buys, not even one

Fucked new…to life…
Jaundiced free, fare free
To Samarkand land…
And all there is – to a market

Is a tree…
To Somorika
Where existence begins in the imagination
And the head is a ghost

Hanging out of the leaves of branches
Crying out kamikamikami** –pluck and die
What is free is not the same, but is not different
From AIDS...WE PAY WITH OUR LIVES...

And words cannot forever go on...

---

*   We are yet to survive
    We are yet to be free
    From the hands
    Of the bitterness of the bitterleaf

    And words
    Harden themselves up
    Words are not bitter to the mouth
    And yet people run away with their mouth closed.

Efuala from efualand
(For Efuala)

What is this land to you
A home away for you to pay up
To you your days for a new life
Better than the old of memories
Better left and forgotten in the old home

And to now make you
"With passion" to hate is hidden
Not from all eyes, you don't know
How to sob on someone in secret
Unseen the touch of flesh before this time
Or is it for there after bitten turned down

Why are your eyes even
With tears for worth ungiven
From those who lie about their pocket
Who would not share with you their lunch
Except in want of something from you

Why pang your heart with a helmet
In quest of the honour due to a prophet
When is this your county
To make the saying into the contrary

When in Efualand
They saw your trueself ringing
A reception into reality
Even in their own Lagos
They cannot equal your feat

From Efualand you came
Leaving all in quest of the better
Don't jump out to start all over again
Let not all these days count into waste
Meek on to all, keep low

The opportunity is coming
To get you and sure and then
Your true worth would be seen
As much as your black skin radiates

Unable to hide

Please don't ever allow goodness
To hide from you

Love no more a poem

Love in me for you
Can no more
A poem

Death then
Is not a wish
But a witch

For flesh bloodful
And bone on my way
To lost you

For only death
Can in me
Wish love die

This country is not a poem

This country is a poem
Is only for the heart to lie
To make Art no die
This country, no be place
For human faces
To live to love this country
Na just like space
For all of us to dey die
My heart no go greee mek Art dey lie
This country is not a poem

The way they make poetry
To make this country
Sound good to the ear
But here who cares
The death of a dirty lie on the lips
Before the words dried out to die
This country

Who cares
For the poetry of our existence
The way they care for poetry
Leaving us every moment with metaphors
To feel not at all the failing of poetry

This country
Dare you to ask
"Have you seen dead bodies before?"
Answer with another ask
'Are there not dead bodies everywhere?'

Stuff enough to make more poems
Who cares to hear
Lagos is a poem, not a place
Cannot sit to hear this poem

Kile ni wa gbo
Kile ni wa wo
Ara mo ri ri
Kilo oju ori leko ri
Kile ni wa gbo
Kile ni wa wo

One arm at swinging
With five fingers of the other
For cover over at play
On the organ whole in the hole
Pressed at pee
Gbamgbam lan tu sokoto

Sokoto Gbamgbam
Eba mi tu Eba mi so
Gbambgamlan
Sokoto Gbamgbam
Eba mi tu Eba mi so
Gbamgbamlan

Dangling in the gbamgbam
Walking naked on the street
Feeding eyes
Who cares for the little flesh
Like worms...
Dieting you from the inside
This country

Lay you down
The way sleep can strip your eyes close
And the bridge becomes the bed
Eko ole bi...who cares
The same way "I am a citizen"
Counts not to this country

Plucking being away from the people
Dying heart out of the flesh

Being the only way love can live
To see eye to this country
Love is free
To suffer the same stew

Dare to care to nurture a mind
Still young
Becomes the undoing…
This country
Cannot grow out my love for you

See how songs squeezed in series
Unending… only to dry them out
Unwet by lips
My fingers have not touched
Unsuckled by your tongue in flesh
Consult with another tongue

How this country steals the care
Out of the heart…
The flesh for …care to feed the future
Suffers love to the same fever
Of sickness

The power of poetry to heal all
So go ahead break the borderline
Invoke afterwards Tracy Chapman
A poet to another
"Sorry…forgive me"

In love nothing can be wrong
Open flesh wide, eating is eating
Even with a friend 'best than your brother'
For the share of some bottles' drunk
Flesh is willing to lie on flesh

Only after to lie with the eyes
But needs can't hide

They speak loud
For those that can read figures to see
In the sealed silences of open sisterly
The munching of lips in the closets

How then do they unreleased
The duet composed on you
When they lay flesh on flesh

Forgiving
–Falls before the freedom of freegiving
Is no necessary effort
It is this country
Stripping people off their hearts

For a lifeless living
Take it or befriend death
What choice has love
Than follow in the lead like
This country, like love

Ending on the pages of a poem
To keep your cherished heart – and die
Blood immingling in the lone country
Of words that keep fate only in fiction
Of faith

Not wanting…. This country
Cannot die for its comedy
Like Gbenga Adeboye
The laughter continues
Atop his own grave, the crowd
Disperses the doubt of Thomas
Unbelievable to beat Jesus' own
3 days after, he resurrected

Even the police are a part of the pact
To bring back to life

Entombed remains of a year old
Nothing is impossican't
Just believe ... in this country
Wonder way ... better than Aliceland

Where else can a body ridden with 29 shots
Read the headlines "road mishap"
Daring who the Poet to say
This country is not a poem
And the letters die unworded
The mouth has other use
To feed, to sing a chorus for the crowd

This country
I sing am say na poem
For any other heart to say na lie
Na to make Art to dey die
This country, if no be place
For human faces
To live to love This country
Wey big and getti space
Abeg na where deadbody for dey see ground dey die
Abeg mek dem carry them heart and art of lie go die
This country
I dey sing am mek yousef dey sing say na poem

Maruwa lo keke....
Na the keke of Maruwa
Use am, dem we use am
Carry millions...
If you no getti chance enter...
Mek you wait
Abeg you mek you wait
This country wey do am
Bring 79 back 99
Go still dey do am for them
Maruwa lo keke
Na the keke of Maruwa

Use am, mek dem dey use am
Carry millions…

This bitch of ocean
We are too many waters merging oil
For its flow families into a union…
And nothing
Nothing for the commonfaces
But the ones in lush luxury
In abundance of unending
Laughter of "life is sweet"
They still eat this country cash of oil
And they kill to keep this country one
And call our dying … love

What love…?
When we pay more than more
In bitterness…
Roasted in flames of pipeburst
Kerosene exploding our commonfaces…
To hang on to life on the beach…
This beach of ocean….
Becomes … the bitch …
This country

Dying us sunrise sunset
In daily dosage….
Scavengers of skull for sale
Not in one full swoop at Sarajevo
Mass unmasked for massacre in mind of Milosevic
Is only a portrait of Polpot like Pinochet
This is what they call politics

There is no better metaphor for death
Other than this country
"Die no dey scarce again" for here
And dying just can't last on forever
And not die…. And when dying is over

It is not death …. Death is over you
Only because this breath is over
There is no heart to this country

This skully bone of no supple flesh
In league with death to disbursing dying
So who cries for this country?
Cannot be me … cannot be the commonfaces
Those who can cry for this country
Are shielded from the stench
Uncountrying the rest of us
To hate this country….

Spaces we cannot make
But places… without people
Remains unmade
In wait for the failed messiah
Awaiting crucifixion
For digging into us in June 12 daggers
Returns to rule…
Where else… Tragedy
Replays in the same name
In the same person
Atiku …ooo….
What difference

For a people mugged down in mud
Every breath a struggle to keep
The breath like that of animals
Humans lost all life … like Hannibal
Desecrate the palace unfit for Villa and Zapata
Hang the statue in the square
This is the sad end of Saddam's story
Still alive savouring life on

Like Bush the liar unable to Blair
The people not to see their land
Their oil still flowing into wrong pockets

Guns boomed, they die to be able to kill
My heart is pained say no be dem
But the innocent young ones of mothers
Like our own mothers
Cut down to weep dry tears
For lost sons

This is the common end of hope
Stringed on the guns of another
From across the borderline
Who also like them heed only onto profit
From our dying
If then we free to fight
This country into a poem
Art first must be rid of lies
For only then can hearts crave to die
For the people
For a new poem
For a new country
Not this stiff old song of profit
Making this country is not a poem.

This country is a poem
Is only for the heart to lie
To make Art no die
This country, no be place
For human faces
To live to love This country
Na just like space
For all of us to dey die
My heart no go greee make Art dey lie
This country is not a poem

How can we count

We can count
Every other thing
But our blood
Unstopping rushing flood

Our blood defies figure fingering
To number words in letters leaving
Us round and round ringing
To death–

The only currency living
With which to exchange existence
To banter for better
How can we count

Our flood flirts with all the seasons
Why there is no ceasing
To live life like this… is death
Now existence

Love another name for murder

If love is to eat dust
I want to die
Away from flesh

If love is to hunger at life
I don't want
To ever eat flesh

How is love the same name for murder

Reading of love

Race me on my flesh
See if I would not bone over
To be all me

Pluck me free from hate
With night wrapped
In close lock

And we then can be
We are not the love
To make

You want to only me me away
From me kill me to you

This is not in my reading
Of love

The way to hate

Nobody tells you the window
You can come in or out
For this unmakes the door
Restoring bending, crouching
Our days as apes

Are beings of all bodies
Not animal?
Our own new name
H-U-M-A-N-B-E-I-N-G-S
Differs us we think

And yet all bodies' needs
Are the same…for the same needs,
Like bodies in need of love to feed
On others flesh bodies, love
Is the very way to hate

Segregation… the body
Cannot make love to another
Animal body, without first
Seeing the head looking like
A look alike

The ashes of the heart

Sex to these some
Opens up the flesh
A book of memories
Of love ... not won
Of heart harvested
Out to others

Chance seeing
For a stealing
Of a momentary
Feel for flesh falling on flesh
We lost to forever make
We rest do

The ashes of the heart
Of others
Leaving slips of sours
Our lives contending not
What can we not do

Open up the flesh
Like a book to read
Of love lost, to win a heart
That today is a cage
And when we break out
Freedom is a past to this country
But not to the people.

Unwrite God

Can the poem not rite
Out the poet?
Lunge on the lung and life out

Can the poem not write
Art
Is meaningless itself not a meaning

Can the poem not right
The heart
To stir feelings capable of everything

Unmaking the maker
The made is what is... writing
God.

Then the poem
Can also unwrite
God.

Kraftgriots
Also in the series (POETRY) *continued*

Paulina Mabajoye: *The Colours of Sunset* (2004)
Segun Adekoya: *Guinea Bites and Sahel Blues* (2004)
Ebi Yeibo: *Maiden Lines* (2004)
Barine Ngaage: *Rhythms of Crisis* (2004)
Funso Aiyejina: *I, The Supreme & Other Poems* (2004)
'Lere Oladitan: *Boolekaja: Lagos Poems 1* (2005)
Seyi Adigun: *Bard on the Shore* (2005)
Famous Dakolo: *A Letter to Flora* (2005)
Olawale Durojaiye: *An African Night* (2005).
Ebinyo Ogbowei: *Let the Honey Run & Other Poems* (2005)
Joe Ushie: *Popular Stand & Other Poems* (2005)
Gbemisola Adeoti: *Naked Soles* (2005)